C

MANHATTAN CARNIVAL

MANHATTAN CARNIVAL
A Dramatic Monologue

By Frederick Feirstein

Preface by
X.J. Kennedy

The Countryman Press
Woodstock, Vermont

Copyright © 1981 by Frederick Feirstein

Introduction © 1981 by X.J. Kennedy

Library of Congress Cataloging in Publication Data

Feirstein, Frederick.
  Manhattan carnival.

  I. Title.
PS3556.E445M3   811'.54   81-3224
ISBN 0-914378-68-6   AACR2
ISBN 0-914378-69-4 (pbk.)

Manufactured in the United States of America

For Linda

ACKNOWLEDGMENTS

Special thanks to CAPS for their grant which helped me complete this book and to the Big Apple Poetry Contest for their Prize.

Sections of MANHATTAN CARNIVAL have appeared in the following magazines:

Green House: "Mark Stern Wakes Up,"
                 "The Garbage Drummer"

The Kenyon Review: "The Street,"   "A Girl,"
                       "The Crash,"   "The Stanhope,"
                       "The Child,"   "The Phone Call,"
                       "The Jeweler,"   "The Zoo,"
                       "The Meeting,"   "The Jukebox"

The National Jewish
        Monthly: "The Windows,"   "The Blind Man,"
                     "Happy"

"CRAZY, WOUNDED, BUT A-MAYING"

In the beginning, you will meet Mark Stern, a man estranged from his wife of ten years, as he wakes up with a nurse he picked up in a bar, a woman given to grisly platitudes. "Doesn't screwing make you feel alive?" she chirps, and at once you know you're in the hands of a master satirist. Few pages of *Manhattan Carnival* didn't make me laugh aloud, and yet the continual laughter has a twinge to it; and it seems almost an incidental reward. For at the center of this astounding poem is a serious insight. In the midst of presentday New York, Frederick Feirstein has fashioned the closest thing to *Tristan and Isolde* we're likely to get — a contemporary story of the torments of love.

Readers unfamiliar with contemporary poetry will feel not the least bit disadvantaged, because they can read *Manhattan Carnival* as readily as though it were a novel and get immediate pleasure out of it. Once they are hooked by the saga of Mark Stern, they will forget that it is told in (of all things) rhyming couplets — five hundred and thirty-three of them. Now it takes high art to make a poet's art invisible, and Frederick Feirstein is not only one of the most highly skilled poets I know, he is probably the least pretentious. Each couplet is a lens to look through. No demonstrations of the poet's technique obstruct your view. But those readers to whom the poem may prove a challenge are those most deeply familiar with contemporary American poetry. For some, it will be necessary to park a few pet assumptions outside. One such assumption is that there is really no point in writing long narrative poetry in this day and age; that the action of storytelling has all moved over into the novel. To hold this received idea, however, is to ignore the pleasures to be found in a work that supplies both poetry and drama simultaneously — pleasures afforded by poets from Homer on, and in our time by poets such as Lowell and Frost. Another critical assumption — almost a cliché — is that rhymed metrical verse cannot possibly capture presentday American (that is, urban) experience. Such verse (the assumption goes) can't be true to the nervous, disconnected rhythms of city life; to the discontinuity of our lives (whatever that is). Now this assumption is a lot of cant, and Feirstein grace-fully demolishes it. The most cursory glance into *Manhattan Carnival* will suggest that more contemporary and urban than it, you cannot get. Consider, for instance, the dialogue alone — the absolute rightness of it, the ear finely tuned to the language of "this stone island." The insults, the kidding: "Watch it, you'll still get old," as a jostled passerby complains. "You always promise, but you never get," says child to mother. Then too, that memorable bit of phone booth graffiti: *For haircuts with a twist, call Dainty Jim.* Setting fuses seamlessly with people and events.

As Stern, his marriage broken, roams New York's streets, he finds in the faces of the crowd a shattered mirror. And perhaps the entire poem implies one huge metaphor: Stern's fractured marriage in many ways is like his relationship to the city itself — painful, wry, comic, occasionally sad, and yet (somehow) fulfilling. The little encounters with strangers, the petty clashes, the reachings-out — these reflect Stern's inner life. His odyssey, rambling as it seems, leads inevitably to a goal, as surely as Joyce's Bloom's tour of Dublin. Stern, for all his hang-ups, is a hero; and it's beautiful to watch how Feirstein brings him home at the end, to discover that "Somehow love remains when love decays." Moments of Stern's travels stay with you — his gratuitous act of pulling a cabbie from a blazing taxi, his being mistaken for a doctor while a jeweler shows him trinkets, his explosion of sexual rage as he contemplates the seals in Central Park Zoo. New York, Stern knows, is necessary to his very existence:

> I need the antiseptic house next door,
> Its plastic shrubs, its missing thirteenth floor,
> Its glass door with its wooden coat of arms,
> Its lobby with its European charms;
> Its French Provincial chairs, its Spanish chest,
> Its walls with scenes of gypsy Bucharest,
> Its German pewter mug and washing bowl;
> Its elevators playing *Barcarole*,

Its terraces where crones play solitaire
Or paint their toes and set their platinum hair,
Its rows of built-in air conditioning vents,
Its windows mirroring the tenements
Across the street, ruins of a better Spring,
Less lonely, rootless, modern, maddening.

This is not even to mention Feirstein's human wisdom, his tenderness, his harrowing honesty. Nor that it seems rare for an immense contemporary poem to be splendid entertainment. Why wait any more? So read, enjoy. Even learn something.

X. J. Kennedy

MANHATTAN CARNIVAL

Mark Stern Wakes Up

"Get up!" "Marlene?" I smell the April rain
And squint half-dreaming at the windowpane
Where winter light intensifies to Spring.
I pull the plug so our alarm won't ring,
Then prop myself up on our double bed
And dip to kiss the imprint of your head
And rub your pillow for Aladdin's lamp.
Oh, I'm a sheltered child away in camp!
Get up, she's gone, "Marriage is for the birds."
But who expresses feelings in *those* words?
Stockings, torn underpants litter the floor.
And who's that leering from our bedroom door?
Some empty-head I picked up in a bar.
Those words — *she* said them last night and, "You're far
Gone hubby. Nurse must bandage baby's heart."
But when she came, I smelled a silent fart.
    Tamed by ten years of marriage, I'm polite.
I cook for her so she can have "a bite"
Before she leaves to do her "nine to five"
And "Doesn't screwing make you feel alive?"
I want you now, I don't want a divorce.
Last night I rode a tourist buggy horse
Around the room where Pegasus once flew.
And infidelity? Of course, taboo.
I let her laughing blow my ear, "Goodbye,
You'll still be married on the day you die."

1

I pace exhausted, though I slept last night.
I watch a jet plane's earnest gray goose flight
Between the roofs: from your apartment here?
I pull a tin ring off a can of beer
And aim the spray against a dirty pane.
Here's to you rain, more promising than rain!
Mark Stern's fizzled out ... What's chirping? I rub
My finger till the window's clean. A shrub
Downstairs is budding — city warts but green.
Sun smears the ivy with a blinding sheen.
The super cranks her clothesline, conjuring
A flowering branch of colored cotton: Spring!
A bluejay leaves her husband's underwear
To soft-shoe through Manhattan's killing air:
A '20's dandy dressed in top hat, tails.
I rap the window with my fingernails,
But he is "on the town," the stupid thing.
This dying city is no place for Spring.
Or am I just emotionally weak?
I scratch the itchy stubble on my cheek
And dash into the bathroom where I piss
And shave and pick my scalp's psoriasis.
I shout into the mirror football cheers:
"You've lived on this stone island thirty years
And loved it for its faults; you are depressed.
Get out, discover it again, get dressed."
    My eye is like a child's; the smog is pot.
Shining cratefuls of plum, peach, apricot
Are flung out of the fruit man's tiny store.
Behind the supermarket glass next door:
Landslides of grapefruit, orange, tangerine,
Persimmon, boysenberry, nectarine.
The florist tilts his giant crayon box
Of yellow roses, daffodils, and phlox.

A Disney sun breaks through, makes toys of trucks
And waddling movers look like Donald Ducks
And joke book captions out of storefront signs:
Cafe du Soir, Austrian Village, Wines.
Pedestrians in olive drabs and grays
Are startled by the sun's kinetic rays,
Then mottled into pointillistic patches.
The light turns green, cars passing hurl out snatches
Of rock-and-roll and Mozart and the weather.
The light turns red. Why aren't we together?

Happy

I hear a tinny racket at my back.
I fantasize a woodpecker's attack.
It's Happy tapping with his coffee cup.
His Yorkville restaurant is opening up.
"What are you doing, writing in a trance?
A dog will lift his leg and ruin your pants."
"I'm waiting for Godot," I want to say.
But then I'd have to summarize the play.
Happy loves theater-talk — "a hit!" "a star!"
And who fucks who and who "the faggots" are.
But knowing that my real concern is art,
He'll ask me how a stunt man does a part,
And so I say, "I'm working on a play
About a star like Lassie who turns gay,
Shows up on the movie set with shaved legs ..."
"Come on, you crazy bastard, ham and eggs?"
He tells me every morning that I'm weird
For marrying "that broad" who charcoaled a beard

And moustache on his Playboy pinup.
And yet he likes you, tells me "Keep your chin up.
She'll find it ain't no picnic by herself."
He asks me to inspect his knickknack shelf
While he cooks: a hard hat hanging from a big
Bottle of beer, a painting of a pig
Entitled "Oink Oink Lib" ... You know I fear
To lose the little contact I get here
If I mocked him? You used to be the friend
I'd wake to. I've hoped that your affair would end
With you alone, implacably regressed.
I've prayed you'd call at 3 A.M. depressed,
Apologizing, begging to come back
— Or else I'd fake a massive cardiac
And call you, "Come and tend me!" God, that nurse
Last night. I hope your 3 A.M.'s are worse!
    The landlord sits a stool away from me.
He needs the contact of my enmity.
Remember how he never speaks, but rants
And wears the same clothes every day: striped pants,
A bowler hat, a gray vest, banker's coat?
His perfume masks the odor of a goat.
Although he's nearly seventy-years-old,
He'd fuck a crone whose crotch was gathering mold.
The tenant in me knows no self-control
But there's a daisy in his buttonhole —
It's Spring! The miser wouldn't buy a rose.
Happy puts down my plate and winks: he knows
My feelings well. (He told me, "Once that crook
Gave me the mouth. I hung him on that hook.")
Then Happy to the landlord, "Now you crumb ..."
The landlord shouts, "You write it down, you bum!"
And Happy pulls his ballpoint from his ear.
The landlord orders, "Your balls fried in beer."

And so it goes — the covert warmth of men:
The landlord ranting, Happy jamming his pen.
   A rotting odor and I spin around.
As if she has been dug out of the ground
The sidewalk tenant licks her filthy hands,
Then spits three times and Happy understands
She needs a buttered roll — for free. Forget
The thanks. This girl was once a majorette.
   She wears a braided blouse, a tasseled hat.
She doesn't walk, she marches, and "his frat"
Are all the words we've ever heard her say.
She grabs her gift. The landlord jokes, "Now pay!"
Her eyes look trapped. She howls like a mute
And, as she flees, he pinches her. "A beaut,
But Schmaltzpuss here can't bring himself to chuck her
Because deep down he really wants to fuck her."
Happy shuffles the puzzled landlord out:
"You choke on hate, you lech, you Sour Kraut! ...
Come on, now eat your eggs, be a good boy."
"They're cold," I say. "They feel like corduroy."
"They're made to eat, not wear, you stupit kit."
I punch his arm, he slaps my cheek, we hit
Farcically, turn the counter into a drum,
Pounding out maddened rhythms till a bum
Enters, sings operatically — he thinks.
Happy says, "It's not your breath alone that stinks."
I feel ashamed but Happy shouts, "Get out!"
The bum stands still with a defiant pout,
But then looks down in terror at his shoes
And cries, "Dear God, I'm losing all my booze!"
   I need the antiseptic house next door,
Its plastic shrubs, its missing thirteenth floor,
Its glass door with its wooden coat of arms,
Its lobby with its European charms;

Its French Provincial chairs, its Spanish chest,
Its walls with scenes of gypsy Bucharest,
Its German pewter mug and washing bowl;
Its elevators playing *Barcarole,*
Its terraces where crones play solitaire
Or paint their toes or set their platinum hair,
Its rows of built-in air conditioning vents,
Its windows mirroring the tenements
Across the street, ruins of a better Spring,
Less lonely, rootless, modern, maddening.

The Street

The street is full of children off to school.
I enter them, swim in a wading pool.
She lugs a briefcase much too big for her.
He throws his hands up at a jabberer.
She beats her chest and howls like an ape.
He shifts his jacket to a Batman cape ...
And all those years we never had a child.
What books I wrote, anthologies compiled!
I walk uphill — a hill! — a concrete maze
Conceals the roots of Spring where sheep might graze,
Where deer might nibble garlic from my hand
And lick the imprint of my wedding band,
Where we might find the time and ease to walk
Kissing, while neighbor cows and weasels gawk.
Maybe we'll walk across a stream on rocks,
Find fields of four-leaf clovers, poppycocks.
If we spent just one month without concrete,
Without the crowd's abrasion, in bare feet,
We'd be so bored, we'd learn to talk to ducks
— And they would say we were a pair of schmucks

To leave Manhattan Island as we know it.
Island? Thank God the concrete doesn't show it.
Instead we have our craziness and fights,
Our block with such cosmopolitan delights
That when we first moved in, I wouldn't go
To eat anywhere but in Mexico
Or France. What dance halls, beer halls, fast-food shops
— So wild at night each corner needs two cops.
Even that bank is lively with its flags,
Its jazz band sitting on heaped moneybags
That read *Grand Opening*! "With every new
Account you get a plastic kangaroo,
A yellow snot!" a dwarf is shouting. "Here's
Two plugs of free wax from an old man's ears!"
— A group of bankers try to shut him up —
"A free electric ... grnf ... a porous cup.
Let go, you mannikins, I'll bite your cocks!"
Then walks off, "Get your free, unnumbered clocks!"

The Cowgirl

   Three bankers with the same suit, haircut, face
Concur that New York City is no place
For living, only work. "To save your health,"
One frames the air, "leave here. To save your wealth,
Bank here." The others whomp him on the back
Exclaiming, "He's a poet! What a knack
For putting all our thinking into words!"
"The ads we have are really for the birds."
— "And bees," The Poet adds. "Right on!" "Here, here!
Where is the pretty lass to spread good cheer?"

A smiling cowgirl dances out on cue.
The Poet hugs "Our Colorado Jew."
She's dressed up in red cowgirl boots and skirt.
She winks at me and laughs, "Ain't he the flirt?"
She wears a crown of tinfoil painted green
— A Jewish Princess turned Homecoming Queen.
    A nervous bank guard with a smoker's hack
Follows, chin barely balancing a stack
Of cups. Then a teller shows off, wrestles out
A giant bird-shaped bottle with a spout
Shaped like a heron's beak. It flattens his nose.
He shrieks, "This juice is freezing! Save my toes!"
    The cowgirl giggles, pets the plastic bird,
And squints to spell its giant, orange word:
"It's P-A-P-A-Y-A, hold that line!"
Her voice, for all its shouting, is a whine.
She hands a plumber eyeing her a cup
Of "Mama Nature's Great Papa-Ya Juice!"
And says to sneering me, "Hey man, hang loose."
"Oy Got," I say, "It's not my cup of tea."
Her smile twitches, but still mechanically
She serves the blushing super from next door
Then, baby-talking, asks the plumber, "More?"
The super coughs, sneezes out his juice,
Apologizes, wants to introduce
His wife to her, open a joint account.
"Not me, I'd rather buy a jewel to *mount*,"
The plumber jokes, tonguing his juicy lips.
The cowgirl cutely shakes her leather hips.
"The Poet" pats her bottom, "You'll go far."
"Not all the way," she prinks. "A movie star,"
I sing-song Yiddish, "you vill never be.
No veed forgets its roots, take it from me."

The cowgirl's face falls dead. She looks like you
When I abused your helplessness. "Yoohoo!"
I call at no one down the block, "Vait up.
This lonely momser got a crazy kup."
    I won't look back. I think I'd turn to salt.
Like them I locked a jewel inside my vault;
The "victim" you, provoking rage for light.
You said that we'd conceive a parasite!
Those words destroyed me. I must eat again,
And like this greedy crew of garbagemen
Scavenge the city for the child in *me*
So long neglected, screaming to be free
Of you my infant wife, neurotic twin.
If I could tell you, where would I begin ...?
Although you said you'd change for your own sake,
You couldn't manage it; I couldn't take
Your clinging mannerisms, baby-talk,
The self-defeated, mincing way you'd walk.
"What do you want? Money from me? For what?"
A girl is tapping on a paper slot:
"A quarter, man. Drug rehabilitation!"
And if *I* plead for reconciliation,
You'll know I'm hooked, as this child was, is still.
She tugs at me to prove she has a will.
I dodge her, Moonies, Socialists, and run
Hard for a bus.

The Blind Man

"10-3-7 Lexington"
— A blind man, ivory cane outstretched, steps in.
His face is handsome with an English chin,
High cheekbones, chiseled nose, eyes marble-white
As if a bird had pecked them of their sight.
His coat is cashmere, Ivy League in cut.
He doesn't weave. He tries a cocky strut
Although the bus jerks out of the stop.
He smacks each hanger like a razor strop.
A woman stands and offers him her seat.
He quickly sits and pulls in dainty feet,
Then pulls an old man to his hearing aid:
"I would appreciate it if you paid
My fare. Is this eight nickels and a dime?"
The old man says, "Of course" in pantomime,
Then toddles forward, toddles slipping back.
And then the blind man opens his attack:
"My name is Paul D. Hartley-Robertson.
Excuse me but I talk to everyone
In buses, toilets, restaurants, and stores.
What work do you do?" Then — without a pause
To hear "A psychoanalyst" — "Oh, yes?
I knew it by your voice. Now you must guess
What job I work at, I am very rich.
My loneliness is like a maddening itch
That I can't scratch, that I can't even find.
The least part of my plight is being blind.
I'd like to phone you. I keep friends that way
Or visit you — at any time of day.
The friends I make in coffee shops or buses
Support my spirit by Bell's rupture trusses."

The old man smiles. The blind man pushes on:
"You'll never guess what I read in the john."
"Oh, *Playboy Magazine.*"
                              "How did you guess?"
The old man purrs an analytic "Yes."
"They make too much of sex. Their jokes are great.
Masters and Johnson I think deprecate
The holy beauty in the act, don't you?
Like children sticking pencils into glue."
The old man laughs, "I think, perhaps, you're right."
"To love is not to have an appetite
For someone's organ like a slab of liver.
Have you read *Portnoy?* God, it makes me shiver.
In other words, no love, no sex.
And you think what? This business is complex."
The old man bends, "Your stop on Lexington."
The blind man: "10-3-7 Robertson,
What's yours?" The old man, silent, pulls him up.
The blind man from his pocket pulls a cup
And smacks it in the old man's guarded face,
Then stumbles off, "You've *queered* another case."
The old man snorts, "A busman's holiday."
His face unmasked is coronary gray.

A Girl

I'm staring at a girl with Chinese hair,
With harpist hands, skin white as a pear.
She's almost you when young. She wears your grace
— As if she's naked in a sheath of lace.
Her sitting still is actually the sum
Of all potential motion. If I come

To you, an older brother, take your hand,
Say when you're insecure I won't demand
You be less innocent than this young girl ...
　　The Seventies behind me in a whirl
Of barbershops and bakeries and banks.
The psychoanalyst leans back and yanks
The signal cord to stop. I'm in the bus
— This toughened Me is so preposterous —
Because I want to be where we began.
I rub my ring scar for a talisman,
Then slam the unlocked door and hurtle out
And, like the shrink, with his defeated pout,
The past's ahead of me — your favorite shops
Awaiting us. I haven't written flops,
You aren't terrified that we are poor,
You don't suggest my pen begin to whore
For advertising agencies and soaps
Or scream, "We can't feed children on your hopes."
　　The world looks simple in these fancy blocks.
There are no grandmothers in army socks
With all their worldly goods in paper bags,
No windows warped or cracked and stuffed with rags.
Instead old mansions, churches, private schools,
And rooftop gardens, rooftop swimming pools.
This market selling jumbo squab and goose,
That florist selling miniature spruce,
This dress shop with its leftist magazines
And racks (here poor is chic) of faded jeans.
We squatted here, pitched pennies at the wall
And through that ladder hooked a basketball.
We bicycled and rowed in Central Park.
We necked, defying muggers, after dark.
We sauntered nibbling sauerkraut like grapes.
When maids or doormen sneered we swayed like apes.
We ran like blind men once for seven blocks,
Both stricken by a midnight urge for lox

And settled for a closing pizza stand
And once ... Your life now? Mine seems second-hand.
I have to call you ... calmly now ... it's dead.
The slot is sealed off with a plug of lead.

The Crash

I hear a crash and turn. A wall of flame
Surrounds a car. I'm hollering your name.
The passersby first freeze, then screaming run.
The burning car is like a loaded gun.
A doorman grabs my belt to hold me back,
"That woman" — Woman! — "must be charcoal black."
I shout, "The cab that hit her .. over there!"
The doorman pleads, "He doesn't have a prayer!"
I pry the door. He's married to the wheel.
He doesn't look alive. I reach to feel
His pulse. "You nut, get out before it blows!"
The cabbie's life is ebbing from his nose.
"Exhaust pipe's catching fire, hurry up!"
I pull him free and make my palm a cup
To stop his bleeding. Someone hugs his feet.
We lug him way past safety down the street.
I'm suddenly in Lenox Hill berserk,
Bellowing at an intern, "Hurry, jerk!"
A fire engine's siren tears the air,
Then hundreds more — lunatics at their hair.
The cabbie's face has dribbled into gray.
I squirm from pats and handshakes, storm away.
I won't look back as hoses douse the pyre.
Remember how my greatest fear was fire?
And if I was a hero, would you love me?
At least, Marlene, you'd think much better of me.

The Stanhope

My lungs are bruised, my ribs are tightened belts,
My eyes are cuts, my sinuses are welts.
I jog to heal them with sulfuric air.
I dodge a dog by leaping up a stair,
Then jitterbug past French and Parke-Bernet.
A woman cries in Bronxite, *"Je ne sais!"*
Another shouts, "Watch it, you'll still get old!"
The New World's paved with dog-shit, not with gold
And tasteless in its art. These galleries
Are filled with junk the touring Japanese
Cart home with moccasins, tin Empire States,
Key chains with footballs, paper license plates.
Let's try this phone. A punk's torn off the dial.
A cabbie greets me with a futile smile:
"There's nothing in this area that's straight.
The City Council sluts should get the gate.
Push-button phones: logical to install?
Instead they push a midtown shoppers' mall
And ruin my business ..." "Sorry, full of smoke,
I've got to run." "This Mayor is a joke!"
He shouts, loping beside me down the block.
"You want to suck a cabbie's twelve-inch cock?"
I pick up speed. I sprint. He falls behind
And panting rasps, "A priest once fucked my mind,
Then shot me naked with a movie lens."
I want to hear the pigeons, squirrels, wrens
— As natural as litter in the park.
I want to see a toy boat disembark
Imaginary insects from the pond
Who strut to Alice, hand poised like a wand.

I want to drink from fountains at the Met.
I want to nibble nuts, sip anisette
Together at The Stanhope's French café
You painted, furred, me sporting a beret.
That was your fantasy, to sit like swells:
Primped, feminine, your thoughts all bagatelles
And me the waiter's tyrant, me John Wayne,
Me Tarzan, you — a Women's Libber — Jane.
   Why didn't I indulge you, play your mother?
Instead I ridiculed you, "Find another
Sugar-daddy. What 'Libber'? You're a kid."
I didn't know how true that was, you did.
A sixty-year-old man in banker's clothes,
His veiny calves, I'm sure, in gartered hose
And in his buttonhole, each day, a rose.
We had an open marriage. My affair
Was with your twin: high cheekbones, long black hair
As all since then have been. That empty head
Last night was you. Does he still share your bed?
   You hear that infant howling, "Feed me, please?"
Your mother's in the kitchen on her knees
And praying to the Virgin for the strength
To discipline you, keep you at arm's length.
Your needs are sins; your kicking, flailing: crimes.
She'll feed you only at appointed times.
And me? My Momma cracked my Poppa's nuts,
Accused him hourly of "chasing sluts."
To keep her still, he decked her out in fur.
Gigantic diamonds, learned to worship her.
I vowed I'd never be a Jewish eunuch.
To nibble nuts here would have been my Munich.

The Greek Revival Houses

Another crash. This time there's no escape.
Helpless I watch as wreckers mug and rape
The Greek Revival houses, one of which
We swore we'd buy when we were old and rich.
Fierce crowbars pry the floorboards' tightened knees
And hammers smash the husband on the frieze
Above the mantel in our living room;
And at the entrance where a stately brougham
Once champed, a metal trough receives the litter;
And in the scaffolding the monkeys titter:
"Who's got the power now to call me 'boy'?"
"Hey, look at this!" "That's Kikey, Jr.'s toy."
"We could get something for it, it's antique."
"The toilet's gone, I gotta take a leak."
"Piss on that wall. I'll hide you with my back."
"Let's see their money hold back this attack.
Bonzai! Go suck my cock, ol' bankrupt Jew."
"Come down and fight!" I shout up, "I mean *you!*"
"What's that?" the pisser cocks a quizzing head
Then, laughing, waves me off, "You punk, drop dead."
"If you can fight as well as you can piss ..."
He shouts, "You're late for your analysis,"
And straining lifts his drill to show his prick
And shuts me up by shattering our brick.

Alice

I pull my shoes and socks off and I race
Past traffic to the park, pick up my pace.
Watch! Dog-shit, one-two, marbles-two, watch! glass.
Step past those adolescents in the grass.
His hand one-two is creeping up her thigh.
Behind, an angry snatch of lullaby:
A nurse one-two shudders her baby carriage.
The girl shouts, "No, I save that for my marriage!"
I have to stop and smell these cherry trees.
Remember when we kissed here on our knees
And touched each others' faces as if blind?
"I only touched your valentine behind!"
Anachronistically she shrinks away.
"I promise you I'll be so good today
The priest would even trust me with his sister."
I smile. The girl spits, "Mind your business, mister."
    I circle Alice with her hybrid band
Of flesh and bronze. She waves a wand-like hand
And March Hare pulls his stopwatch from his coat.
A little bully grabs him by the throat
Till his eyes bulge at the mouse with giant ears.
Fat twins shoot up imaginary spears
At Cheshire Cat half-hid inside a tree.
Their tiny sister, white with jeopardy,
Crawls among the lizard, worm, and snail.
Another girl tries frantically to scale
Alice's mushroom throne. The sun
Blazes, turns all of them to gold. I run
To where Hans Christian Andersen is reading
The Ugly Duckling. He is also feeding

The ugly duckling. Children mob his lap.
One climbs his book and pulls a Yankee cap
Over his eyes. I read, "Gold fields ... green oats."
A girl shouts, "Betcha fifteen cents it floats,"
Snatches the cap, flings it into the pond.
The boy jumps in, a beauty, platinum blond.
He's followed by a setter and a stick.
"Come on, you rat, I only want a lick!"
The girl tiptoes her ice-cream out of reach
And taunts her younger brother, "Jump, you leech."
   One-two uphill past chestnut-vendors, cops,
A soccer game, two deaf boys spinning tops.
An old man in a wheelchair, halved by stroke,
Tips his tweed cap at me, "Keep it up, bloke!"
I pick up speed for him. "Good show," he smiles.
I have the energy to run for miles.

The Child

   "Get natural Italian ices, cuz,"
A vendor shouts, "I'm licensed by the fuzz!"
Beside him a balloon man with a grey
Rocket of helium makes a bouquet
Of purple, orange, yellow, white, and pink.
The ices-man, "Get also orange drink!"
A tourist wearing giveaway white gloves,
A straw hat with a pin of turtle doves,
Asks for the flavors in a Southern drawl.
The ices-man snaps, "Just one left, that's all."
"A typical New Yorker," she replies.
Stunned by those words, tears welling in his eyes,

He lifts her hand and kisses it. "For you
— For free! dear lady, take my special brew."
She sucks a cup of all his remnants mixed.
A rainbow "Typical New York" has fixed.
She walks away perplexed: is this one mad?
He beams, "Two years an immigrant, not bad!"
But no one else will buy his rainbow ice.
   "Here's white balloons with little colored mice
Right in them, see?" "Mommy, oh please!" "Not now!"
"You always promise, but you never get."
"Sometimes, you know, a person must forget
His pleasures." "Why?" "Because you are a brat."
"What did I do?" "You've taken off your hat
To spite me." "But it's warming up, it's Spring!"
"You've disobeyed me, you can't have a thing."
"I'll keep it on for one balloon — a deal?"
"No bargains with the devil." "Pleeease!" "Pigs squeal."
She wrings her pocket for a cigarette.
"Society," I say, "will pay your debt
In violence." "What!" she screams, her ears blood-red.
"Don't spoil your child," I say. "Creepo? ... Drop dead!"
I walk away. I want the child to follow.
And for a decade — why! — your womb was hollow.
   I lose myself in an uproarious crowd.
Although a sign reads, "No Feeding Allowed,"
A squat gorilla nonchalantly licks
A rainbow ice, and then to spice it up he picks
His nose — "Gorilla sprinkles!" — the crowd loves it,
Then twists the cup and through the mesh he shoves it.
"That means the ape wants more!" "Another cup!"
That mother runs to buy one, "Fill 'er up!"
And glares at me, triumphant. The crowd cheers
When, in their midst, torch high she reappears.

Above the ape house our native bird
The pigeon sits, too shocked to say a word.
The tiger weathervane turns frantically.
The wrens explode in an apostrophe.
The squirrels, suicidal, pace the cage.
The child in me, *my* child, berserk with rage
Buys all the white balloons and colored mice
And hands them to the child, "For being nice,"
And to the mother, "Let me buy this gift."
She glares triumphant once again. I drift
To where the parrots and macaws shriek color.
A keeper stirring coffee with a cruller
Says, "Saw that, pal. That woman's for the birds.
A month ago, the two of us had words.
This hand all on its own became a fist.
It took religious training to resist."
He shakes his crotch, "With this we'd make her learn
What kids are made of, huh?" I smile and turn
Away. A seal, a human amputee,
Suns on her back with a serenity
That turns her to a mermaid with a trunk
So sensual I'd want to fuck, if drunk
— Not drunk, I want my prick to be a tongue
Demanding flowers grow in this world's dung.
I want to fuck that giddy nine-year-old,
Her hair a sheet of Rumpelstiltskin gold.
That seal's mouth must be like a baby's cunt.
I want to make the female grizzly grunt
And watch the tigers in the darkness mate
And urge the baby gnu to masturbate
And kiss each waitress in the park café,
Then prance among the patrons, flagrantly gay.
Not even fantasies would we allow.
Why when we married did we make that vow
Of even thought-fidelity, Marlene?
To drive each other crazy was obscene.

The Garbage Drummer

I try to find a clearing on a bench
Crowded with chattering Japanese and French
And more are coming down the thoroughfare
From lobbies in The Plaza and Pierre.
A native shifts to make a spot for me.
I thank him but he's lost in melody,
Shaking his head, his eyes glazed, fingers popping.
Though he is sitting, he is Lindy-hopping.
His partner is a black attaché case.
He has a criminal, a killer face:
Low forehead, tiny ears, scarcely a chin,
Long greaseball hair, a leopard's hungry grin.
He wears a dirty white shirt, white silk tie,
Cufflinks of broken lapis lazuli.
His pants are pegged. He wears a cowboy belt;
A sort of sheath of brown rain-stiffened felt
Hangs from a loop. He eyes his watch, then booms
"It's Showtime! Gather round ye brides and grooms!"
He draws two drumsticks from his sheath, then runs
From bench to bench, "Come on, you mother's sons,
It's Showtime!" But the tourists shrug and smile.
The thoroughfare becomes a nightclub aisle.
He overturns an empty garbage can.
A tourist shouts, "A New York hooligan!"
A cheer goes up. He takes it for applause,
Then lifts his hands high for the crowd to pause.
He lays his case upon the can — a drum.
He twirls his sticks and then sings out, "Ta Dum!
The style of that great genius Buddy Rich,
A style which I can imitate, but which

Cannot be stolen, it's a signature.
But study will transform the amateur
To this ..." His sticks start rapping with such skill
I feel a '40's bobbysoxer's thrill.
I know his face. He was a famous man.
It's ... who? reduced behind that garbage can.
"It's Krupa now. You recognize that beat?"
I'm clapping, shouting "Bravo" on my feet.
The stupid crowd is cheering with derision.
The drummer stops, "We'll have an intermission."
The sneering crowd throws coins. He picks them up
And humbly mutters, "I must get a cup."
"You're brilliant, man," I say, "So why this gig?"
"They catch you forging checks when you get big."
    He turns to beg. I realize he's me,
Childishly giving work away for free.
At first it seemed to suffer was romantic.
Who dreamt of being anxious, laughed at, frantic?
Or, fearing the imprisonment of work,
My father in his bank cage, petty clerk,
His moral dicta: *compromise and grin.*
A man is one who keeps his feelings in
Until he doesn't feel. Survive! Survive!
A man is one who seems to be alive.
The garbage drummer shouts, "You folks must pay
To keep my self-respect, or I won't play."
A Frenchman drops a coin, pinches his cheek.
Who cares for art? The drummer is a freak.
"I will not be an advertising whore!"
I wanted to be taken care of, poor
Enough to make my father right, a man!
We lived inside a mirrored garbage can.
Each day I grew more passive, you more wild.
The child is only father of the child.

The Phone Call

And so to phone you, I must search these blocks
Outside the park where men are peddling clocks
That have no time for them, their dress-shop grins
As wooden as their wooden mannikins,
Must search for one phone not ripped out in rage,
One booth that's not a puked-in bank clerk's cage.
If I must contact you through plastic, steel,
Then you must listen to my choked appeal
— "My choked appeal"?! I leave the booth and walk
Away. If we can't meet, at least let's talk.
I dial your working number ... seven ... five
Connect! This trembling makes me feel alive.
"Hello! ... Who's this? ... Mark Stern ... Marlene
Of course ... But where? ... She's not in quarantine! ...
Then tell her I will call back after three."
Your long lunch is with whom? Of course you're free
To have a mid-day fuck. Your friend at work
Told me — her intonation was a smirk.
But I will search the delis. God, I'm nuts!
"And right in front of me, pulls out his putz,"
— A shopgirl tells this to a clucking friend —
"He says, 'If you go down for me I'll spend ...'
I think this creep is listening in." "Who cares?"
I shrug. She says, "You want to buy my wares?"
"I'm looking for some corned beef and a knish,"
I say. "I'm sure that's just your kind of dish,"
She says, I say, she says, I'm stalling, scared.
If you are not alone, then I'll go mad.
If you're still nibbling on his pickle ... "What!"
"I bet your wife has tied it in a knot."

The street seems tilted as I walk — not here.
"I'm sorry. Take this, buy another beer."
I'm knocking people down. No phone here ... "Hey!"
"I'm sorry, pal, I meant to spit away."
I hate this Spring, rebirth, no birth, this city.
I hate my monomania, self-pity.
I hate that Hasid, hate his button shop.
I hate that jeweler, hate that traffic cop.
I hate the Gotham Bookmart, Berger's Deli.
I hate this clothing salesman's massive belly.
"I'll take corned beef on rye, but slice it thin ..."
(I'm dieting for you.) "With saccharine."

Art

"As for the soundness of these recent goods
You're pushing for the ski slopes and the woods
I think, my friend, you're steering way off course.
The snow would drench them through and through. A horse
Would give you such a rash that I suggest
You change your line, forget about the West."
    " 'A liberated woman would wear slacks!'
My dear, his nineteenth-century attacks
Have left you with assertions that a mouse
Makes to a cat, and *should you clean your house?*
It's his, his bed, his lamp, his barbeque,
His toilet paper, t.v. set, his you!
Your analyst? He rapes — you clean — your mind.
I recommend you bed down with your kind."
    "The standards, rules by which a business runs ...
(The tongue is mine, the blintzes are my son's.)
I claim him, yes, despite his clothes and hair
— And goals ... No, I won't practice laissez-faire,

Not with your future on the line. You'll find
That 'Art' looks good to you because you're blind.
Fashion determines *what* books will be taken,
Not talent ... No, I'm trying to awaken
Your common sense. You're not a woman, black
Or Eskimo, you're not a dwarf. Attack
Minorities? I know the world, you schmuck.
Ethics? It's all manipulation, luck."
I whisper, "Sonny boy, your father's right.
You have to have a business sense to write,
To know what fashion will be in this year
Or, how to ease the current guilt or fear.
Just like a whore you must be versatile
Yet witless, cliché-ridden, juvenile."
    The father laughs. My younger self replies,
"Polonius was confident and wise.
You write, I have no doubt." "But what?"
"Porno films." "No." "Soap operas." "Guess." "A lot
Of Broadway shit that makes *him* feel secure."
"Oh no, I'm idealistic and obscure."
He laughs, he has a nervous high-pitched cackle:
"Your book is in the Holy Tabernacle."
"Okay, you guessed it. All I write is crap.
You must be as intuitive as ..." I snap
My fingers as his father would and wink.
This aesthete takes my cue, "I'm sure you stink."
"You've seen my work?" "Who needs to?" "Hack work?" "Yes."
"I see it in the corny way you dress."
"Checkmate!" the father smiles and grabs his bill.
The son sardonic, "What a bitter pill."
    The father's watch-alarm goes off. You're in!
The phone booth's empty. How shall I begin?
"I lap Sephardic cunts, my tongue is choice ..."
"Marlene?" ... *Call 6* ... You recognize my voice!

"I want to meet ... Yes, hard to make the call ...
You name it ... Five ... The Exxon Building Mall."
"For haircuts with a twist, call Dainty Jim."
Just tell me this, are you still fucking him!
"I can't talk either till we're face to face.
Five, then." I'm just eighteen, squatting to race
Nine other track stars for the City Cup.
"Another nickel, sir, your time is up."
The gun goes off ... "Marlene?" I thought I won,
Danced a jig in triumph. Then, "Hold it, son.
You had a false start." We begin again.
I come in second, win a fountain pen
Which six years later brings me you — Forget?
In that dead time a poet, sick, in debt
Was sexy, spiritual. Now he's what?
Francine (The Muse) is marketing her *"twat."*
   A woman with my mother's fed-up smirk
Intones, "This ain't no library, you jerk."
"Pardòn," I say, a Frenchman wedging out.
My brows are tense, my mouth a Gallic pout.
"Une map, n'est-ce pas? Dee-rections à la Church?"
She pushes past me in a manic lurch
To "Mark?" she calls. "It's Marlene, schmuck, his wife."
I swear, Marlene, upon my mother's life
This hag, this nag, that partner of the schmuck
Bear both our names. I watch her, horror-struck.
A honey tongue, a heart of gall ... "Some nut
Is looking at me, Mark!" The booth slams shut
... Is fancy's spring, but sorrow's fall. Decay
Is really happening to us. "Cherchez
Les femmes elsewhere!" she shouts, covering the phone.
I can't live out my agonies alone.

The Jeweler

I dash out where a thousand watches say
It's 4:15, you're thirty-five today.
Oh no, I'm all potential, I'm eighteen
And charming, carefree. Am I not, Marlene?
You see yon tray of jewels, my faithless Queen?
Shall one grace your pale bosom or your ear?
A jeweler crooks his finger, "Come in here.
I've got the lowest prices on the street.
I know what you want. This one's most discreet."
He holds a ruby pendant to the light.
"The treasure of an exiled Muscovite."
I snort, he smiles — "A doctor, like my son."
"A what?" I ask. "Don't fake. I know it from
The hippie way you dress. It's your day off
I know, but I can't leave here and this cough ..."
He opens up a mouth of onion soup.
"My day off, mister." "Does it look like croup?
I'll pay for diagnosis! What's your price?"
"That simple wedding band." "It's very nice."
"Could you inscribe it?" "Yes." *"Forever five ..."*
"That's cute." " *...The only way to keep alive.*"
"I think you're a psychiatrist." "You're right."
"The grandson of an exiled Muscovite."
I wince, he laughs — "The ring for one small peek,"
Then like a father slaps me on the cheek.
His tongue is ugly, geographical.
"Say *Ahh* ... Your problem is — electrical."
"What's that!" he shouts. "You like the girls?" "Of course."
"Your wife?" "You ever see a milkman's horse?
— Except no milkman takes her off my hands."
"Did you once buy each other wedding bands?"

28

"I think all you psychiatrists are nuts."
"Your throat is sore from sticking in your putz."
"You mean The Clap?" he claps his forehead, "No!"
"I mean, too much can make resistance low."
His eyes are panicked, wild birds in a cage.
I realize your lover is his age.
"Doctor, how long must I abstain?" "A week."
Relieved, he slaps me lightly on the cheek.
"I'll have your ring inscribed in half an hour.
My wife, I used to call her 'City Flower.' "
I leave him hands clasped, weeping at your ring.
The traffic noise outside is deafening.

The Windows

I need the windows of the Tourist Boards
On Fifth — their beaches, lower Alps, and fiords —
The students playing clarinet duets,
The mime in top silk hat and epaulettes,
The Hari Krishnas spreading incense, joy,
Their flowing peach robes, shoes of corduroy,
The blind man singing hymns, St. Thomas Church,
The scaffolding where whistling workmen perch,
The haughty English manager of Cook's,
St. Patrick's nave, Rizzoli's picture books,
Tiffany's clock, the pools of Steuben glass,
The pocket park with cobblestones for grass.
Remember how we'd stroll on your lunch hour?
My nickname for you then was "City Flower."

I turn towards Sixth, past two construction sites,
Through crowds. A girl in ballet shoes and tights
Pirouettes down the block, her raised hands moths.
"You want my stock of English terrycloths?"
"A smart guy puts his money in a bank."
"So when I told him that his foreplay stank ..."
A drill starts up. "Big dildos, two bucks!" Where
Are you, Marlene? "He told me, '*You* are square!' "
The girl is in a swan's pose, lifted up.
The crowd applauds. The blind man shakes his cup,
Protesting joy. The crowd moves on. Marlene,
Are you here somewhere in this Zanuck scene?
　　Under this thin shattering crust of stone,
A train is roaring, "You must die alone."
But I can't live alone, with silent nights,
Without the heat and contact of our fights,
With anonymity, trapped in my time,
Communicating like a "glassed-in" mime.
The air is cut by helicopter blades
Above these glacial skyscrapers, cascades
Of workers, blue-faced, trapped at their machines.
I'd love to blow this block to smithereens,
Especially that emblem of our age
The Hotel Hilton, concentrate my rage
Upon one Building Trades conventioneer,
Give him a New York City souvenir.

The Marriage Counselor

"If you've a marriage contract, do not burn it!"
A man armored in placards grabs my wrist.
"Without some order, Man cannot exist."
He points to the same adage on his hat.
"I went to court and filed a caveat
Against divorce, until I could be heard
Exposing Women's Lib as less absurd
Than sinful, yes, against Our Lord's intent,
For marriage is a holy sacrament!
A thousand people all across this nation
Have signed my plea for Husband Liberation:
From washing his own dishes, socks and hair,
From seeing women working everywhere
While he is unemployed and she wants money
— Court-ordered, Queen Bee ordering her honey."
"I half-agree," I say, "but have to go."
"What half?" he says. "A man must cock and crow."
"I have to meet my former ... friend at five."
"A half-a-man is only half alive."
"I understand your plight." "My what?" "Your pain."
"It's Man's right, not just Woman's to complain."
I wince. He follows me. "I'll bend your ear
Only a second more. You want to hear
A joke? If crazy Women's Liberation
Would undergo a brain operation,
They'd call it minor surgery. You've heard
That women always get the final word?
He fought his shrew for fifty years, then died
Only to have the slab bought by his bride

Read 'Rest In Peace — Until We Meet Again.'
Sign here for Husband Sufferage! Are we men
Or mice? One captain, pilot, driver, king.
A family like a team needs managing.
A woman's place, God says, is in the home.
He wrote that in The Book and chromosome."

The Meeting

These lights are slow. I'm going to be late.
I still have Broadway's hordes to navigate.
Come on you red-eyed cyclops, change! "Curse who?
I'm talking to the traffic light, not you."
"Stop thief!" a hooker tugs me, as I dart
Through pimps and Johns. If we are forced apart
By this old lady's poodle ... "Sorry, wait
Till I catch my breath ... You cut your hair? ... Looks great."
I want to ruffle it and say It's *me*
And stop this small-talk, this formality
Of gesture, tone of voice ... "The Theater's dead
As usual." I want to take your head
Between my hands and touch your non-stop tongue
With mine — as on this New Year's Eve I hung
A mistletoe above your photograph
And kissed ... I haven't heard that nervous laugh
For months. "Why did I call today? It's Spring!
Let's talk in there." (Damn, I forgot the ring!)
    "This place is awful. Ceilings like a bank.
Enormous champagne bottles. And this swank
Wallpaper from the thirties! Even time
Is marketed these days. Jesus, now I'm

Chattering nervously — like our first date.
Waiter? We'll both have the roast beef hot plate
(Just as we had it then), coffee with cream ...
I ordered without asking from a dream,
Not from my 'piggish maleness.' Oh Marlene,
Stop preaching. We're repeating our last scene:
You breathing hard from Libber's rage, not passion,
Me mocking my arch-enemy: Fashion.
Please, let's pretend we're not destroyed by time
Or social change. A man is in his prime
At thirty-five and, God, I feel half-dead,
Reduced by half, like our half-empty bed ...
　　I haven't slept around much — funny phrase —
Although it is like sleeping: sex, these days ...
Thank God you left him! ... How could I have guessed? ...
You thought an open marriage suited *me*?
I lied to you to save some dignity! ...
I've needed you no more than I need breath ...
Of course I'm changing — quickly into death.
I need two children sucking at your tits.
I need each mortal inch of you, your fits
Of baby-talking, bargain-hunting; fears
Of poorhouse, workhouse, welfare ... I'm all ears.
Loneliness makes me blabber ... I feel
That too about you, that you had to *steal*
Affection ... Don't call yourself 'a bourgeoise bitch,
A hypocrite!' You needed something rich
To nourish you. I couldn't ease your hunger ...
I don't know why he needed someone younger! ...
I want to go home too. You leave the tip.
Forget your guilt ... Pfft, taxi! On my lip?
— It's ketchup. Kiss it off. I hailed him first!
Don't touch that handle ... *You* will get the worst!

You coward — hit and run! Don't cry. Let's walk
Like innocents again across New York.
Let's swagger, arm in waist through Central Park,
And neck defying muggers after dark
And saunter nibbling sauerkraut like grapes.
Let's take our shoes off, shirts off, pants off, traipse
Like infants — parodying our worst and best.
Take off your melacholy, get undressed ...
I'm serious. We'll let our bodies talk
While neighbor elephants and pigeons gawk ...

The Zoo

I know that you were 'acting out' — don't cry.
My wound is healed. That cage is empty — why? ...
Kids beat the deer? With sticks? This ugly age:
They ought to stick the public in that cage ...
It isn't hurt. It's terrified of us.
Come here, my love, we too are timorous
Of our civilized aggression, quick
Confused outbursts; no talk, no warning — stick!
You want to cry about this year beat dead?
I didn't change the linen on our bed
For seven months — and you used paper plates
Whenever you ate in? These two are mates.
They can't intuit what hostility
Can suddenly erupt from us in bed
Because your schizophrenic mother fed
You pet food when her schedules broke down,
Because my drunken father tried to drown

My cat with bourbon in the sink, because
I dream of Harpo in a cat's mask, claws
Flaying my father's back, because his wrists
Are really scarred, because two analysts
And seven thousand dollars couldn't stop
Your mother masturbating with a mop
Or mine from comforting her twelve-year-old
Half-lost in nightmare, terrified and cold,
By slipping into bed with him, until
He woke with an erection, broken will.
And yet it's Spring again and we're forgiven.
And if I swear to you that when I'm driven
By guilt and fear to make my tongue a stick,
I'll realize I'm mother's lunatic;
Will you when starved for milk not love please swear
You won't suck off that cow-eyed millionaire?
You see those cherry blossoms bridesmaid white,
Those bluejays half-embracing, half in flight,
These pigeons shameless in their mating-dance?
We have to give ourselves another chance.
And next year after failure, give another.
Let's have that child. You're stronger than your mother.
Whose hopes, intentions aren't ruined by time?
And chronologically we're in our prime.
In other words Corinna what I'm saying:
We're crazy, wounded, but we are a-maying.
    These animals are growling for their meat.
Robins are pulling earthworms from concrete.
The Delacorte clock's chiming, 'It is sunset.
Stop jabbering, divorce is not undone yet.'
Come on, let's leave this park, this pubic place
Between the bowed legs of Manhattan, race

That doorman to a cab ... This driver's mad,
Hold tight! The curbstone's not a launching-pad!
— Or else we're in a farce, that rear-end Death.
He means to shave its paint. Let out your breath.
But close your eyes — he's squirting through two trucks.
They rebound off each other. 'Got the fucks!'
Mack Sennett hunches over. 'Now a cop!'
We want to walk a little, driver, stop
Right here! We're nearly welded to that bus.
Don't throw that horse laugh at us — Pegasus.

The Jukebox

This antique store is new. They keep their stuff
Out on the street at night — the owner's tough.
Look at this view of Sheepshead Bay with schooners ...
Carney and Gleason in *The Honeymooners*.
That campaign button's whose? My eyes are weak.
They're bringing out a jukebox — *that's* antique,
At least as old as me ... He owns the shop.
Are you attracted to him? ... No, I'll stop.
Of course enjoy your fantasy! Her ass?
Too flabby for me, but her tits ... The glass
Is lighting up. What record's wobbling down?
It's Benny Goodman and *Sweet Georgia Brown*.
Look at the crowd that's gathering. I'll bet
This derelict once played the clarinet.
He's tightening the air — his ligature.
His bitter, toothless smile is his armature.
This pimply girl dressed up in Grandma's style
Is awed. 'He beats Ted Lewis by a mile!'

I'll bet this Catskill type in houndstooth pants
Will ask that snazzy meter maid to dance.
You see that woman fussing with her hat?
She's getting set to foxtrot with her cat.
You hear her? 'Play a slow one!' There she goes
To Nat King Cole. She's stumbling on her toes:
A ballerina broken by Relief?
The couple waltzing with the handkerchief
Between them are engaged Hasidic Jews.
The crowd ignores the dwarf peddling *The News*
Of murders, bombings, chaos, doomsday, time.
We're innocent, let's dance. The only crime
Is coyness, lady. Let the sun collapse
And night come, we must shoot our craps
Once more, must challenge Death to play.
The jukebox blinks. The song is *Yesterday.*
    A traffic helicopter overhead
Reports that you're refusing to be led
Even in celebration, reports the crowd
Is laughing at us arguing out loud
That you should lead, that I think in clichés,
That somehow love remains when love decays,
Reports a man is falling to one knee
And shouting, 'Marlene, please re-marry me!'
Reports that you are crying 'Yes No Yes,'
Reports that I'm unzippering your dress
And leading you to bed, that you're without
Your diaphragm, 'Let's have it now!' I shout,
That you shout back, we're coupling like rhyme,
Reports that we're oblivious to time.
I'm coming — do you hear that baby crying
Across the garden where the wash is drying?"

Manhattan Carnival is Frederick Feirstein's second book. *Survivors,* his first book of poems, was selected as an Outstanding Book of 1975-1976 by *Choice,* the American Library Association Magazine. He was a Guggenheim Fellow in poetry for 1979-1980. In 1977 he won a CAPS Award, The Poetry Society of America's John Masefield Award, and a Big Apple Poetry Prize.